A BUSINESS APPROACH TO CANNABIS FARMING

Complete Entrepreneurial Step By Step Guide To Cannabis Garden From Scratch

I0427359

ZHURI HART

DISCLAIMER

This book is intended to provide general information and insights on adopting a business approach to farming. The content within is based on the author's knowledge and experiences up to the date of publication. It is essential to recognize that the field of agriculture is dynamic, influenced by various factors such as market conditions, climate, and regulatory changes.

Readers are advised to conduct thorough research, seek professional advice, and consider their unique circumstances before implementing any strategies or practices discussed in this book. The author and publisher disclaim any responsibility for the accuracy, completeness, or suitability of the information provided. The book is not a substitute for professional advice, and the author and publisher shall not be liable for any damages or losses arising from the use or reliance on the information presented herein.

Individual results may vary, and success in farming enterprises is contingent upon numerous variables. The author encourages readers to consult with relevant experts, agricultural extension services, and legal or financial professionals to tailor strategies to their specific needs and local conditions.

This book is not intended to be a comprehensive guide to all aspects of farming, and readers should exercise their judgment and discretion in applying the principles discussed. The author and publisher do not endorse any specific products, services, or companies mentioned in this book unless explicitly stated.

By reading this book, the reader acknowledges and accepts the inherent uncertainties in agricultural endeavors and agrees to use the information at their own risk.

TABLE OF CONTENTS

ABOUT THE BOOK

"A Business Approach to Cannabis Farming," a book, fills a vital need in the fast-changing market by providing thorough information. The book establishes the scene in the introduction by exploring the history and development of the cannabis industry, describing its goals and parameters, and pinpointing its intended readership. Readers are better prepared for the in-depth investigation that follows with this core understanding.

"Understanding the Cannabis Industry," gives readers a basic understanding of the cannabis plant, its background, and the current trends in the local and international markets. It also looks at the regulatory environment, which is an important topic for any entrepreneur figuring out the complexities of the cannabis industry.

The book delves into the business side of cannabis production. "Business Planning and Strategy" offers insightful guidance on how to define a cannabis-growing enterprise, carry out market research, create a strong business strategy, and take legal and regulatory considerations into account. This chapter emphasizes how crucial a well-considered strategy is to guarantee sustained success.

Cannabis cultivation's practical aspects are covered. The book "Cultivation Practices" walks readers through important choices such as strain choice, cultivation techniques, and environmentally friendly farming methods. "Facility Design and Equipment" offers guidance on how to create productive farming facilities, decide between indoor and greenhouse arrangements, and incorporate technology for maximum yields.

"Financial Management and Funding," the focus is mostly on the financial side, and readers are taken through financial compliance, income estimates, budgeting, and funding choices. With a strategic financial focus, readers are guaranteed to be well-equipped to make decisions that support the expansion and sustainability of their cannabis farming endeavors.

Equally important topics including distribution and supply chain management, marketing and branding, and legal and regulatory compliance are covered. Every one of these chapters functions as a thorough manual, providing helpful tips and tactics for overcoming obstacles and seizing chances in the ever-changing cannabis sector.

"Challenges and Opportunities," which discusses typical problems that cannabis growers confront, offers case studies of prosperous companies, and offers an outlook on industry trends for the future. With its methodical and thorough approach, the book is set to become a vital tool for professionals, investors, and business owners considering a career in cannabis farming.

CHAPTER ONE

CANNABIS FARMING INTRODUCTION

THE HISTORY AND DEVELOPMENT OF THE CANNABIS SECTOR

Over time, the cannabis business has experienced a remarkable transformation, moving from a stigmatized and illegal market to a thriving legal one with enormous economic potential. The cannabis industry has a complex route towards public acceptance, partly because of its deeply ingrained cultural, social, and political background.

Cannabis has been utilized historically for a wide range of uses, from industrial to therapeutic to spiritual. Due to its psychotropic qualities, it has frequently been outlawed, which has resulted in a decades-long illegal market. However, the industry has undergone significant change as a result of shifting public perceptions and an increasing amount of scientific research demonstrating the plant's medicinal benefits.

COMPREHENDING THE CANNABIS SECTOR

Investigating the complex nature of the plant and its derivatives is necessary to comprehend the cannabis industry. Cannabis sativa, the formal name for the cannabis plant, is a multipurpose herbaceous plant that has more than one hundred different chemicals called cannabinoids. The most well-known and researched of these are cannabidiol (CBD) and tetrahydrocannabinol (THC). These substances affect several physiological processes by interacting with the endocannabinoid system in the human body.

AN HISTORICAL ANGLE

Cannabis has been cultivated for thousands of years, and historical evidence points to its use for both medicinal and recreational purposes in ancient cultures. The herb has had a lasting impression on human history by traveling across many cultures and being used in everything from ancient Egyptian ceremonies to ancient Chinese medicine.

Cannabis was more recently linked to counterculture movements in the 20th century, which helped to create social stigma and legislative limitations.

CURRENT TRENDS IN GLOBAL AND REGIONAL MARKETS

There is a paradigm change occurring in the cannabis market in the current global landscape. The cannabis business is expanding quickly as a result of the drug's increasing legalization in many nations for both medical and recreational use. A strong local and international market has emerged as a result of the demand for cannabis and its derivatives. The regulatory frameworks of different nations and regions have an impact on the dynamics and growth of the industry.

An examination of the market's current patterns indicates that consumer interest, investment, and innovation in the cannabis industry are all on the rise. The market now includes a wide range of products, such as edibles, oils, and wellness items, and is no longer limited to the production and distribution of cannabis.

Furthermore, the sector has advanced due to technological developments in product creation, extraction methods, and cultivation practices.

THE REGULATORY ENVIRONMENT

Understanding the intricate regulatory environment that oversees the cannabis industry's operations is also necessary for navigating it. Countries and even regions within a single nation have vastly distinct sets of regulations. Aspects including cultivation, distribution, sale, and consumption are governed by the legislative framework, which affects market dynamics and shapes the tactics used by industry participants.

To sum up, the history and development of the cannabis industry demonstrate an incredible journey from illegality to universal acceptance.

CHAPTER TWO

PLANNING AND STRATEGY FOR BUSINESSES

IDENTIFYING THE PURPOSE OF YOUR CANNABIS FARM

Clearly defining the mission, values, and primary goals of a cannabis-growing enterprise is essential when starting a new enterprise. This entails determining the market niche that the company hopes to fill in the cannabis sector, such as cultivating cannabis for recreational or medicinal uses or concentrating on particular strains. Defining the business also means stating the target market, the size of the activities, and the USPs that differentiate the cannabis farm from rivals. To give a blueprint for the entire business planning process, this foundational stage is essential.

RESEARCH AND ANALYSIS OF THE MARKET

The foundation of a prosperous cannabis farming operation is extensive market research and analysis.

Comprehending customer behavior, market trends, and the competitive environment is crucial for making well-informed judgments. This entails investigating regional preferences, prospective development locations, and the market for particular cannabis products. To further identify possibilities and problems in the market, regulatory environment, distribution channels, and pricing dynamics analysis are critical. Businesses can ensure a more robust and adaptive approach by customizing their plans to match market demands through thorough research.

CREATING A BUSINESS STRATEGY

Creating a strong business plan is essential to a cannabis farming venture's success. The company's objectives, organizational structure, marketing strategy, financial forecasts, and risk management procedures are all described in this document. A well-written business plan acts as the organization's road map, assisting in obtaining capital, luring in partners, and directing daily operations. A thorough explanation of the entire cultivation process, from seed to harvest, should be included, along with details about tools, technology, and resource distribution. A well-crafted business plan plays a crucial role in guiding the cannabis farm towards both profitable and sustainable growth.

LEGAL AND REGULATORY FACTORS TO CONSIDER

Effectively navigating the intricate legal and regulatory terrain associated with cannabis cultivation is a crucial component of company planning. It is crucial to comprehend and abide by these laws given the various federal and state requirements. This entails acquiring the required authorizations and licenses, abiding by cultivation regulations, and keeping up with any modifications to the law. Inadequate attention to legal issues may have dire repercussions, including fines or closures. To guarantee that the company complies with the law, a comprehensive evaluation of the legal system and the involvement of legal experts are therefore essential.

EVALUATION OF RISK AND STRATEGIES FOR MITIGATION

Given the many unknowns and difficulties faced by the cannabis cultivation industry, risk assessment is a crucial component of strategic planning. Proactive management requires the identification of prospective risks, whether they are associated with changes in regulations, market volatility, or environmental issues. To reduce risks' negative effects on the company, mitigation solutions must be developed as soon as they are discovered. This could entail getting insurance coverage, creating backup plans, or diversifying cultivation techniques. A carefully considered risk management plan increases the company's overall resilience to changing market conditions while protecting it from future setbacks.

CHAPTER THREE

AGRICULTURAL METHODS

SELECTING THE BEST STRAINS OF CANNABIS

Selecting the best cannabis strains is essential to cultivation procedures because it has a big impact on the end product's potency, yield, and quality. This selection method heavily weighs factors including intended effects, growing circumstances, and environment. While Sativa strains are linked to higher levels of energy and creativity, indicia strains are recognized for their calming effects. By striking a middle ground between these two extremes, hybrid strains give growers a wide range of alternatives to suit their unique needs and tastes.

COMPARING INDOOR AND OUTDOOR CULTIVATION

Cannabis farmers must make a fundamental decision about indoor vs. outdoor cultivation, as each has pros and cons of its own. Higher yields and year-round production are made possible by indoor cultivation's greater control over environmental variables like temperature, humidity, and light cycles. In contrast, outdoor agriculture makes use of the sun's energy to grow plants that may be larger while also using less energy. The space, money, and experience of the cultivator are generally the deciding factors when choosing between the two techniques.

SUSTAINABLE AND CONSCIENTIOUS FARMING METHODS

The cannabis business has witnessed a surge in the significance of sustainable and responsible farming practices because of environmental concerns and consumer desire for products made ethically. To reduce their environmental impact, cultivators are adopting organic farming practices, using renewable energy sources, and conserving water. Adopting sustainable procedures improves the final cannabis product's overall quality and purity while also helping the environment.

PEST CONTROL, NUTRIENTS, AND SOIL

The management of pests, fertilizers, and soil is essential to the success of cannabis farming. To get the best possible plant health and growth, cultivators must carefully analyze the pH levels, nutrient content, and composition of the soil. Using organic soil amendments and fertilizers helps to create a more organic, chemical-free environment. Companion planting and the introduction of beneficial insects are two effective pest management techniques that help preserve crops without using hazardous chemicals that may degrade the quality of the finished product.

METHODS OF HARVESTING AND PROCESSING

The final cannabis product's strength, flavor, and general quality can all be greatly impacted by the methods used throughout the crucial harvesting and processing stages. When it comes to harvesting, timing is everything. If you harvest too early or too late, your yield may be less than ideal or its THC content may decrease. For the terpene profile to be preserved and the overall consumer experience to be improved, proper drying and curing procedures are necessary. Furthermore, proper post-harvest management and storage contribute to preserving the final product's potency and freshness.

Careful consideration of a variety of aspects is necessary for successful cannabis growing, from choosing the best strains and cultivation techniques to adopting sustainable practices and putting in place efficient soil and pest management systems. Meticulousness in the cultivation and extraction processes guarantees the creation of premium cannabis that satisfies consumer and environmental requirements. Through ethical and creative cultivating techniques, cultivators are essential to the future development of the cannabis business.

CHAPTER FOUR

EQUIPMENT AND FACILITY DESIGN
CREATING A ROBUST CANNABIS FARM

A careful approach that takes into account several variables is necessary to design an effective cannabis farm and guarantee the best possible production results. Selecting between indoor and greenhouse facilities is one of the main factors to be taken into account.

Every strategy has particular advantages and disadvantages. Greenhouses exploit solar radiation to their advantage, offering an affordable solution that encourages environmentally friendly farming methods.

However, indoor spaces provide more control over environmental factors like lighting, humidity, and temperature, making year-round cultivation possible regardless of outside circumstances.

CRUCIAL CANNABIS CULTIVATION EQUIPMENT

The success of a cannabis farm is greatly dependent on the choice of necessary equipment. To ensure adequate airflow, avoid the accumulation of pathogens, and guarantee a healthy growing environment, proper ventilation systems are crucial. Excellent lighting is essential for photosynthesis and overall plant development, whether it comes from artificial lighting indoors or natural sunshine in greenhouses. The efficiency of the cultivation process is further enhanced by accurate irrigation systems, fertilizer delivery systems, and monitoring technologies, which guarantee that plants receive the resources they require at every stage of growth.

USING TECHNOLOGY TO ENSURE MAXIMUM YIELD

Modern cannabis production places a strong emphasis on technology integration to increase productivity and efficiency. Real-time adjustments based on environmental variables are made possible by automated systems, such as irrigation and climate control. Modern monitoring tools, such as sensors and data analytics, offer insightful information about the health of plants and enable prompt action to resolve possible problems. Utilizing specialist software for inventory tracking, crop management, and compliance monitoring is another way that technology integration can streamline operations and guarantee compliance with regulations.

INDOOR VS. GREENHOUSE SPACES

The particular objectives and limitations of the cannabis farm are generally the deciding factors when choosing between indoor and greenhouse cultivation facilities. Using natural resources to cultivate cannabis effectively, greenhouses provide a balance between environmental sustainability and cost-effectiveness. Indoor facilities, on the other hand, offer the capacity to precisely regulate growing conditions, permitting year-round cultivation and the generation of reliable, high-quality crops. The decision made between these two solutions should be in line with the cannabis farm's overall goals and strategy.

A cannabis farm's design must carefully take into account elements including the type of facility, necessary equipment, and technological integration. The cultivation process begins with the decision between indoor and greenhouse facilities, each of which has advantages and disadvantages of its own. Using cutting-edge machinery and technology guarantees an efficient and productive growing process, which eventually results in increased yields and better-quality products. For cultivators hoping to succeed in this fast-paced and cutthroat market, they must keep up with the newest advancements in facility design and technology.

CHAPTER FIVE

FUNDING AND FINANCIAL MANAGEMENT

CREATING A CANNABIS FARM BUDGET

In the cannabis farming sector, where accuracy and planning are critical for long-term operations, budgeting is an integral part of financial management. The budget in the context of cannabis cultivation includes several components, including personnel, equipment expenditures, marketing, regulatory compliance, and cultivation costs. Precise financial planning aids cannabis growers in allocating resources efficiently, guaranteeing that they possess the requisite funds for production, processing, and distribution.

Special considerations apply to cannabis production, such as adherence to strict laws and quality assurance requirements. Budgeting needs to take compliance-related costs like testing, license fees, and following cultivation guidelines into consideration. Furthermore, to protect the crops and adhere to legal requirements, adequate thought must be given to security measures, which are a crucial component of the budget.

FINANCIAL FORECASTING AND REVENUE PROJECTIONS

Cannabis growing is a volatile industry with unpredictable regulations, thus income estimates and financial planning need to be done carefully. Estimating the potential yield, market demand, and price swings is necessary for accurate revenue estimates. Because of the constantly changing legal environment and the difficulty of financial planning, cannabis producers must keep up with any changes to the law that may influence their sources of income.

When making financial forecasts, variables including shifting customer preferences, market competition, and macroeconomic developments must be considered. Furthermore, the incorporation of technological tools like data analytics and market research can improve the precision of revenue forecasts. Cannabis farmers can take advantage of opportunities, reduce risks, and make well-informed decisions in a market that is constantly changing with the help of effective financial forecasting.

INVESTMENT PLANS AND FINANCING OPTIONS

Cannabis growing frequently necessitates a large initial outlay, therefore it's critical to investigate a variety of financial sources and investing techniques. The legal status of cannabis in certain jurisdictions may present issues for traditional sources, such as bank loans. In the cannabis business, alternative funding sources like crowd funding, venture capital, and private equity have grown in popularity.

Risk tolerance, growth potential, and the regulatory environment are all important factors to take into account when developing investment plans for cannabis growing. To maximize knowledge and resources, entrepreneurs can choose joint ventures or strategic alliances. Additionally, keeping up with government subsidies and incentives for legal and sustainable farming methods will help create a more stable and diverse funding plan.

REPORTING AND COMPLIANCE WITH FINANCIALS

A responsible cannabis farming enterprise must adhere to financial compliance because the industry is highly regulated. Beyond the act of cultivation, compliance includes paying taxes, keeping track of finances, and following local, state, and federal laws. Cannabis growers need to be accountable and transparent, which means keeping thorough records.

Understanding accounting standards and industry-specific regulations is essential for financial reporting in the cannabis business. Establishing trust with stakeholders, such as investors, regulators, and consumers, requires accurate and timely reporting. Additionally, to stay out of trouble legally and protect the long-term sustainability of the cannabis cultivation industry, compliance with financial and tax regulations is essential.

CHAPTER SIX

PROMOTION AND IDENTITY

CREATING A POWERFUL BRAND IN THE CANNABIS SECTOR

Creating a powerful brand is essential for success in the cannabis sector given how quickly the market is changing and how competitive it is. More goes into developing a distinctive and memorable brand identity than simply coming up with a catchy logo or package design. It calls for a thorough comprehension of the intended audience, familiarity with industry rules, and a dedication to providing work of consistently high caliber.

Cultivating a unique brand personality is one of the most important components of creating a powerful brand in the cannabis sector. A distinct and genuine brand persona facilitates building a relationship with customers, whether the company is positioned as a champion of innovation, wellness, or luxury. Furthermore, cultivating openness regarding product sourcing, farming practices, and testing protocols helps to earn the trust of customers who are becoming more picky about the provenance and caliber of cannabis products.

In the cannabis industry, community outreach and education are two more crucial components of brand promotion. Stereotypes about the industry can be dispelled by presenting a responsible and positive image in the community.

This can be accomplished by taking part in community activities, contributing to charitable organizations, and disseminating informational materials regarding the advantages and appropriate usage of cannabis.

CANNABIS PRODUCT MARKETING TECHNIQUES

Developing marketing plans for cannabis goods that work requires navigating a challenging regulatory landscape and targeting a wide range of potential customers.

Because traditional advertising channels could be limited, firms need to look into other options. In the cannabis industry, content production, digital marketing, and strategic alliances are essential components of a winning marketing plan.

Influencer marketing is one tactic that has become popular in the cannabis industry. Establishing a partnership with influencers that share the values and target audience of the company can aid in expanding its reach and enhancing its trust.

When laws allow, brands can interact with customers through social media platforms, disseminate educational materials, and create a community around their products.

In the digital age, having a strong web presence is essential, and this is particularly true for cannabis goods. Brand exposure and accessibility are enhanced by an e-commerce platform, an engaging social media profile, and an intuitive and user-friendly website. By putting search engine optimization (SEO) techniques into practice, the brand is certain to be quickly found by prospective buyers looking for cannabis product information.

ONLINE PRESENCE AND DIGITAL MARKETING

In the cannabis business, where traditional advertising channels are frequently banned, digital marketing is essential. Reaching the target audience and increasing brand awareness requires establishing a strong online presence. Cannabis firms may reach a wider audience by utilizing many digital marketing channels, including social media, search engine marketing, and content marketing.

Social media sites are excellent resources for interacting with the cannabis community and cultivating brand evangelists. But to stay out of trouble, you have to follow the rules that apply to your particular site.

By adding to the ongoing conversation around cannabis, content marketing—which takes the form of blogs, videos, and educational materials—positions the brand as a thought leader in the sector and strengthens brand authority.

Making sure that a cannabis brand can be found in internet searches requires search engine optimization or SEO. By putting SEO best practices into practice, websites become more visible and generate organic traffic, which eventually leads to conversions. When allowed by regulations, paid advertising can also be carefully used to target particular regions and demographics.

RELATIONSHIP MANAGEMENT WITH CUSTOMERS

Any business that wants to succeed needs to have an effective customer relationship management (CRM) system in place. In the cannabis market, where client loyalty is crucial, this is even more important. Positive client relationships require constant interaction, communication, and attention in addition to the initial transaction.

Cannabis brands may monitor consumer interactions, preferences, and comments by putting in place a CRM system. This information is crucial for customizing marketing campaigns, creating targeted promotions, and quickly responding to consumer concerns. Actively communicating with clients via social media, email marketing, and newsletters encourages a feeling of community and loyalty.

Effective customer service is essential for CRM to succeed in the cannabis sector. A great customer experience is enhanced by prompt and helpful answers to questions, open communication regarding changes or availability of products, and a dedication to problem-solving. Prioritizing client happiness increases a brand's likelihood of gaining word-of-mouth referrals and repeat business—two essential components in the cutthroat cannabis industry.

CHAPTER SEVEN

SUPPLY CHAIN AND DISTRIBUTION

GETTING AROUND THE CANNABIS DISTRIBUTION CHAINS

Because cannabis is a unique commodity with legal frameworks around its distribution, navigating the channels in this field requires a diverse strategy.

Cannabis must carefully choose its distribution routes because it is governed by many laws. Common channels for distribution include wholesalers, delivery services, and dispensaries.

Online platforms and direct-to-consumer business strategies have also grown in popularity. Businesses must comprehend local regulatory restrictions, customer preferences, and market dynamics to successfully navigate various channels. The best distribution plan is also determined by taking into account factors including product potency, shelf life, and packaging.

REGULATIONS AND CONFORMANCE IN DISTRIBUTION

In the cannabis distribution space, compliance and regulations are crucial since the sector is frequently governed by strict regulatory frameworks. These rules cover product testing, labeling, licensing requirements, and shipping procedures.

It takes careful attention to detail to navigate this complicated terrain and guarantee compliance with local, state, and federal laws. Keeping up with changing legal standards is essential because breaking them can have serious repercussions.

Businesses involved in the distribution of cannabis require reliable systems to keep an eye on changes in regulations and respond quickly. Putting in place a thorough compliance policy not only protects companies but also increases industry credibility and consumer trust.

TOP SUPPLY CHAIN MANAGEMENT TECHNIQUES

Successful supply chain management is essential for any distribution network to function, and the cannabis sector is no different. Supply chain management best practices include developing strong channels of communication with suppliers and distributors, utilizing sophisticated forecasting tools, and optimizing inventory levels.

Effective logistics and shipping solutions are crucial since cannabis goods are perishable. Using technology to track in real-time and analyze data helps improve supply chain visibility. A robust and adaptable supply chain system can be established by working with reputable suppliers, using sustainable practices, and implementing agile approaches.

Sustaining a competitive advantage and responding to market shifts need constant observation and development.

CREATING STRATEGIC ALLIANCES

In the cannabis business, forming strategic alliances is essential to successful distribution. By working together, supply chain participants like manufacturers, shipping companies, and growers can improve efficiency and build a more unified distribution network. Establishing strategic partnerships with stakeholders that have similar goals and beliefs can have positive effects on both parties. Since group efforts frequently have more sway over lobbying and compliance activities, partnerships can also help manage regulatory hurdles. Building enduring connections with mutual respect and objectives in mind helps the supply chain feel more stable, which makes it easier to adjust to difficulties and shifts in the market. In the end, strategic alliances can help a cannabis distribution company remain successful and sustainable overall.

CHAPTER EIGHT

COMPLIANCE WITH LAWS AND REGULATIONS

COMPREHENDING CANNABIS LEGISLATION AND POLICIES

Understanding and navigating the complicated world of cannabis rules and regulations is essential when it comes to legal and regulatory compliance. Businesses in the cannabis market need to stay up to date on the latest legislative developments as the industry's legal position changes on a worldwide scale. These regulations include a wide range of topics, such as production, marketing, distribution, and consumption. To guarantee compliance and prevent legal repercussions, enterprises must fully understand the nuances of local, regional, and federal cannabis rules.

PERMITS AND LICENSES

Obtaining the necessary licenses and permits is an essential first step for any company involved in the cannabis sector. Depending on the jurisdiction, licensing requirements might vary greatly, therefore it's important to follow the rules to stay out of legal trouble.

Obtaining licenses requires completing a difficult application process, fulfilling strict requirements, and proving that you have followed certain rules. Whether a company needs a distribution permit, retail license, or cultivation license, it must strictly adhere to the legal framework to function lawfully and win over customers and regulatory bodies.

ADHERENCE TO THE STANDARDS FOR HEALTH AND SAFETY

In the cannabis industry, following health and safety regulations is essential to legal and regulatory compliance. Maintaining the integrity of the supply chain and safeguarding customers require ensuring product safety from the point of cultivation to the point of consumption. Adherence to regulations controlling the use of pesticides and other agricultural practices, as well as stringent testing and labeling requirements, are necessary to ensure compliance with health and safety standards. This dedication not only protects the general public's health but also improves the standing of companies in the sector, building confidence with both regulators and customers.

HANDLING CHANGING REGULATORY LANDSCAPES

The cannabis industry's regulatory environment is fluid and always changing. Businesses in the cannabis industry are always faced with the task of navigating ever-changing regulatory frameworks. It is imperative to be up to date on legislation updates, policy changes, and new trends to effectively adjust to the evolving regulatory landscape. To stay in compliance with changing regulations and take advantage of emerging opportunities, businesses need to be flexible in adapting their procedures. This flexibility guarantees the durability and sustainability of companies in a sector where regulations are changing quickly.

Ensuring legal and regulatory compliance in the cannabis sector necessitates a multimodal strategy that includes knowing intricate laws, securing the required permits, adhering to strict health and safety guidelines, and skillfully navigating dynamic regulatory landscapes. Companies that put compliance first not only reduce legal risks but also advance the general expansion and credibility of the cannabis sector.

CHAPTER NINE

POSSIBILITIES AND DIFFICULTIES

COMMON OBSTACLES IN THE GROWING OF CANNABIS

Numerous obstacles that cannabis farmers must overcome could impede the expansion and financial success of companies in the sector. The intricate and constantly changing regulatory environment about cannabis growing is one major obstacle. Cannabis is allowed in a wide range of jurisdictions, which causes regulatory uncertainty and compliance problems for cultivators. It takes ongoing attention to detail and flexibility to negotiate these legal difficulties.

The absence of standardized technologies and cultivation methods in the cannabis sector is another prevalent issue. In contrast to conventional crops, cannabis production does not yet have widely recognized best practices, which makes it challenging for growers to maximize productivity and yield stability. This lack of knowledge is a challenge to growers of all experience levels who want to increase yield and quality.

Managing diseases and pests is another difficulty in cannabis production. Due to the vulnerability of cannabis plants to a wide range of pests and illnesses, farmers must use effective pest management strategies while strictly adhering to chemical laws.

Maintaining compliance with regulations while managing pests effectively is a sensitive endeavor that requires constant attention.

RECENT ADVANCEMENTS AND OUTLOOK

The cannabis sector is evolving quickly, and several new developments present enormous growth potential. The growing acceptance and legalization of cannabis for both medical and recreational purposes around the globe is one noteworthy trend. Because of this change in public opinion, entrepreneurs now have new markets and ways to profit from the rising demand for cannabis products.

Technological developments are also a major factor in the transformation of cannabis. Cannabis growing is becoming more sustainable, efficient, and consistent because of innovations like precision agriculture, data analytics, and automated cultivation systems. Businesses that use these technologies to their advantage will have a competitive advantage.

Another encouraging development is the growing acceptance of non-traditional cannabis products like edibles, extracts, and topicals.

Businesses can reach a wider customer base and take advantage of changing consumer tastes by diversifying their product offerings. Collaborations between cannabis companies and well-known brands from other industries become more common as the industry matures, creating new opportunities for growth and market expansion.

CASE STUDIES OF PROFITABLE CANNABIS ENTERPRISES

Analyzing case studies of prosperous cannabis companies offers insightful information about the tactics and elements that made them successful. The prosperity of businesses that place a high priority on sustainability and eco-friendly operations is one noteworthy example.

Growers who use environmentally friendly agricultural techniques not only attract eco-aware customers but also reap financial and legal benefits.

Additionally, companies that have successfully handled compliance problems and regulatory obstacles highlight how important it is to remain knowledgeable and flexible. To minimize risks and potential setbacks and to guarantee that they operate within the parameters of evolving rules, successful cannabis companies frequently invest in strong legal teams and compliance systems.

Furthermore, in the cutthroat cannabis industry, companies that prioritize branding and product innovation have become more well-known. Strategic marketing efforts, attractive packaging, and innovative product development all help to build brand awareness and customer loyalty. Growing a strong brand identity is essential for cannabis companies who want to stand out in a crowded industry.

PROSPECTS FOR THE CANNABIS SECTOR IN THE FUTURE

Driven by continued legalization attempts, shifting consumer attitudes, and technology breakthroughs, the cannabis sector appears to have a bright future. The worldwide cannabis market is anticipated to grow as more nations and jurisdictions legalize the drug, offering new chances for companies operating throughout the whole supply chain.

Growing numbers of people are turning to cannabis products for both recreational and therapeutic uses as a result of the ongoing decriminalization of cannabis usage and the rise of wellness trends. A dynamic market environment will likely be created by this changing demand, which will encourage product innovation and diversity.

Furthermore, it's expected that collaboration and collaborations will increase as cannabis becomes more integrated into mainstream businesses like pharmaceuticals, food and beverage, and cosmetics. As legal restrictions get less onerous, well-established businesses from different industries might look at cannabis-related prospects, which would spur additional market expansion and consolidation.

The cannabis sector offers a wealth of chances for innovation, expansion, and success, but it also presents several obstacles that call for flexibility and strategic preparation. Businesses are likely to prosper in this dynamic and changing landscape as the sector evolves if they embrace emerging trends, take lessons from successful case studies, and position themselves for the developing future perspective.